CW00494788

IMAGES OF WAR

THE WAFFEN-SS IN COMBAT

RARE PHOTOGRAPHS FROM WARTIME ARCHIVES

IMAGES OF WAR

THE WAFFEN-SS

OMBAT

FROM WARTIME ARCHIVES

RRUTHERS

Pen & Sword

MILITARY

This edition published Great Britain in 2015 and reprinted in 2021 by

Pen & Sword Military
An imprint of
Pen & Sword Books Ltd.
47 Church Street
Barnsley
South Yorkshire
S70 2AS

ISBN: 9781473833531

A CIP catalogue record for this book is available from the British Library.

Printed and bound in England
By CPI Group (UK) Ltd., Croydon, CR0 4YY

FSC www.fsc.org
MIX
Paper from responsible sources
FSC® C013604

Pen & Sword Books Ltd. incorporates the imprints of Pen & Sword Aviation, Pen & Sword Family History, Pen & Sword Maritime, Pen & Sword Military, Pen & Sword Discover y, Pen & Sword Politics, Pen & Sword Atlas, Pen & Sword Archaeology, Wharncliffe Local History, Wharncliffe True Crime, Wharncliffe Transport, Pen & Sword Select, Pen & Sword Military Classics, Leo Cooper, The Praetorian Press, Claymore Press, Remember When, Seaforth Publishing and Frontline Publishing

For a complete list of Pen & Sword titles please contact

PEN & SWORD BOOKS LIMITED
47 Church Street, Barnsley, South Yorkshire, S70 2AS, England
E-mail: enquiries@pen-and-sword.co.uk
Website: www.pen-and-sword.co.uk

Contents

Chapter One

The Waffen-SS in the West 1940

The photographs appearing in the first part of this book were originally published in the spring of 1941. These images were created under the direction of *Hauptsturmführer* Gunter d'Alquen, commander of the *SS Propaganda Kompanie* and editor of the official SS paper, *Das Schwarze Korps*.

In January of 1940 an *SS-Kriegsberichter-Kompanie* (Waffen-SS war reporters company) was established, and its *züge* (platoons) were attached to the four main Waffen-SS combat formations that fought in the Western Campaign of May and June, 1940. These platoons also remained with their respective divisions for the Balkans Campaign in the spring of 1941. D'Alquen himself was a distinguished SS war reporter and served in the front lines during 1939 and 1940. In 1944 he was appointed by Himmler as head of the entire *Wehrmacht* propaganda department. Among the books he published was an official history of the SS, and a volume originally entitled *'Waffen-SS im Westen'* (1941), the photographs from Chapter 1 of this book appeared in that volume.

Gunter d'Alquen commanded the *SS-Kriegsberichter* unit throughout the war. By 1940 he had attained the *Allgemeine-SS* rank of *Standartenführer*, but began his Waffen-SS command in 1940 as a Waffen-SS *Hauptsturmführer der Reserve*. During the course of the war, he rose through the ranks until he became a Waffen-SS *Standartenführer der Reserve* and exercised the equivalent of regimental command. D'Alquen was responsible for a large back room staff, which processed the incoming material, as well as the front line photographers, movie cameramen, writers, broadcaster and recorders, who served in the front lines. The *Kreigsberichte* in the field were assigned to the various platoons for variable periods of service. Where possible, non-Germans served with their own national formations, but were sometimes detached to cover a particular campaign and report specifically for their own domestic press.

After the war d'Alquen found it difficult to escape his past. In July 1955 he was fined DM 60,000 by a Berlin denazification court and deprived of all civic rights for a period of three years and debarred from drawing an allowance or pension from public funds. The court found him guilty of having played an important role in the Third Reich, of war propaganda, incitement against the churches, the Jews and foreign countries, and incitement to murder. He was judged to have glorified the Waffen-SS, the Nazi State and reinforced the legend of Hitler's infallibility, he was also adjudged to bring democracy into contempt and encouraged anti-Semitism. After a further investigation into his earnings from Nazi propaganda, d'Alquen was fined another DM 28,000 by the Berlin denazification court on 7 January, 1958. He died in 1998.

Many of the photographs featured here feature the men of Waffen-SS *Standarte Germania*. In 1940 the men who bore the word *Germania* on their cuff bands were fighting as a motorised regiment under the command of *SS-Standartenführer* Karl-Maria Demelhuber.

Originally *Germania* was formed in August 1934, as *SS-Standarte III*. It was soon renamed *SS-Standarte II* when Hitler ordered that *SS-Leibstandarte* Adolf Hitler would not be included in the SS numbering sequence. At the 1936 Nürnberg Rally, *SS-Standarte II* was officially granted the honour title *Germania* where it received the unit colours and authority to wear the cuff band bearing the unit title. It subsequently took a part in the annexation of Austria and was responsible for security during the Italian leader Benito Mussolini's visit to Germany. *Germania* also took part in the annexation of Sudetenland. It later served as a guard regiment in Prague, as *Wach-Regiment des Reichsprotektors von Böhmen und Mähren*, until July 1939.

In August 1939 Adolf Hitler, in preparation for *Fall Weiss*, placed the SS-VT under the operational command of the OKW. At the outbreak of hostilities in Poland, there were four SS armed regiments in existence *Leibstandarte*, *Deutschland*, *Germania* and the new regiment from Austria named *Der Führer*, however *Der Führer* was not yet combat-ready and played no part in the Polish campaign. Events during the Invasion of Poland raised a political furore with OKW expressing doubts over the combat effectiveness of the SS-VT. Their courage and willingness to fight was never in any doubt; but at times they were almost too eager for action and this naïve enthusiasm led to disproportionately high casualties. The OKW reported that the SS-VT had unnecessarily exposed themselves to risks and acted recklessly, incurring far heavier losses than Army troops and endangering the achievement of operational mission objectives as a result. It was also strongly argued by OKW that the SS-VT was poorly trained and many of its officers were unsuitable for command. In retaliation the SS-VT argued strongly that it had been mishandled and was hampered by its deployment as sub-units intermixed with regular *Wehrmacht* forces. Himmler took issue with the fact that SS-VT units were fighting piecemeal with the mixed *Wehrmacht* / SS Panzer Division *Kempf* instead of as one SS-VT formation. The SS-VT he argued was also improperly equipped to carry out some of the tasks, which had been allocated of it.

As a result of the controversy Heinrich Himmler, as always, sought to achieve a political end and insisted that, in future, the SS-VT should be allowed to fight only in the form of its own discrete formations, under its own commanders and high command. The OKW reacted strongly to this nonsensical suggestion and in response mounted an attempt to have the SS-VT disbanded altogether. Hitler was unwilling to consider this, but neither did he wish to upset the Army and he chose a conciliatory path. Hitler ordered that for the campaign in the West the SS-VT should form its own self-contained

Division, but this Division and all subsequent Waffen-SS divisions would still come under Army command.

Accordingly in October 1939, the *Deutschland, Germania, Der Führer* and various support units including artillery and reconnaissance battalions were reorganised into the *SS-Verfügungs* Division (SS-VT). Initially the men of SS *Leibstandarte* were earmarked to form part of the formation but the decision was rescinded and SS *Leibstandarte* did not fight alongside the other units. The *SS-Verfüngungs* Division which took part in *Fall Gelb* came under the command of *Generalleutnant der* Waffen-SS Paul 'Papa' Hausser and took part in the Campaigns in the West against the Low Countries and France in 1940. This time round the SS-VT distinguished itself in combat and was to win praise from OKW. The SS reconnaissance battalion played a distinguished role in the campaign and many of the photographs in this book feature that formation.

The SS-VT first saw action in the main drive for the Dutch central front and Rotterdam and many of those images are presented in this book. After Rotterdam had been captured, the Division, along with other divisions, intercepted a French force and forced them back to the area of Zeeland and Antwerp. The SS-VT were next used to mop-up small pockets of resistance in the areas already captured by the German advance. The Division was then transferred to France. Despite Hitler's express orders to halt, Sepp Deitrich ordered an advance by his SS *Leibstandarte* which breached the strongly defended La Bassée canal line, but at a high cost in Waffen-SS casualties. Meanwhile the SS-VT Division finally participated in the drive on Paris. At the end of the campaign, it had advanced all the way to the Spanish Frontier.

The *SS-Verfügungs* Division was later to gain far greater fame when it was re-named as the Waffen-SS Division *Das Reich*. However *SS Germania* had no role to play in that particular formation. The victorious campaign in the West had proved the fighting reputation of the Waffen-SS, and in the process had also opened new and fertile recruiting grounds among the populations of the conquered territories many of whom were sympathetic to the aims of National Socialism. The low countries in particular were to prove a very strong recruiting ground for the Waffen-SS. Initially there were so many volunteers that a new regiment, *Westland*, was quickly formed and its ranks almost immediately filled by Dutch and Belgian volunteers. This was followed by a sister regiment, known as *Nordland*, which was formed from the ranks of Norwegian and Danish volunteers.

Soon after the French campaign, *Germania* was detached from the SS-VT Division and combined with these two new foreign formations, to form the new 5th SS Division comprised of *Westland, Nordland* and *Germania*. The division was originally entitled *Germania* but in order to better reflect its origins it was soon redesignated as the 5th SS Division *Wiking* and was destined to become one of the most controversial fighting formations of the war.

The SS *Aufklärungsabteilung* (Reconnaissance Battalion) was a key component of the SS-VT Division structure, playing a vital part in the French campaign. One of the chief tasks allocated to this fast moving and highly mobile force was to maintain contact with retreating enemy forces.

The BMW R75 was the powerful and highly reliable motorcycle, which equipped the *Aufklärungsabteilung*. The addition of the sidecar meant that three men could be transported on each machine, which gave the unit the advantage of mobility with added firepower.

In May 1940 the SS-VT was on alert for the commencement of *Fall Gelb* (Operation Yellow), which would signal a pre-emptive invasion of the Netherlands and Belgium. The SS Reconnaissance Battalion and the *Der Führer* Regiment received their movement orders first and on 9 May were detached from the SS-VT Division and moved near the Dutch border, with the remainder of the division remaining behind the lines in Munster.

In the first campaign of the war the SS-VT was equipped with the highly effective MG 34. It could be operated as a light machine gun using its integral bipod stand, which was mounted underneath the barrel, or turned into a heavy machine gun by the simple expedient of mounting the gun on a tripod. However, the MG 34 in combat conditions proved to be somewhat over engineered which rendered the MG 34 vulnerable to stoppage at crucial moments. The practical rate of fire in light machine gun mode was around 100-200 rounds per minute. Tripod mounted in heavy machine gun mode the effective rate of fire was 300 rounds per minute. The effective range in light machine gun mode was 600-800 yards, rising to 2,000-2,500 yards in heavy machine gun mode.

Elements of the SS-VT Division first saw action in Holland at 5:35 a.m. on 10 May 1940 when *Der Führer* and the SS *Aufklärungsabteilung* captured Arnhem and advanced towards Utrecht. The reconnaissance battalion had been split into five groups consisting of a motorcycle platoon and two armoured cars each and tasked with capturing an intact bridge over the Maas-Waal canal.

Assault Teams One and Three failed to achieve their objectives and Team One sustained heavy casualties after the bridge at Neerbosch was blown by retreating Dutch forces. However assault teams Two and Four succeeded in securing crossing points at Hatert and Heumen respectively.

The following day, the remainder of the SS-VT Division in three March columns crossed into Holland ordered to penetrate the Grebbe defence line then spearhead the thrust towards Rotterdam. Dutch resistance was expected to be protracted making the assault a costly prospect, however *Der Führer* regiment attacked the heavily defended Grebbe mountain position after a heavy artillery bombardment and captured their objective by 1900 hrs on 12 May 1940.

The fighting in Holland is often viewed as being one sided and half hearted from the point of view of the Dutch forces. However, the *Der Führer* regiment in particular suffered very heavy casualties in the first few days amounting to over four hundred with one hundred and twenty killed and two hundred and fifty wounded by 12 May.

For the Holland campaign, the SS *Leibstandarte Adolf Hitler*, had been incorporated into the Army's 27th Infantry Division and on 10 May spearheaded the northern flank German advance. The SS *Totenkopf* and SS *Polizei* Divisions were held in reserve. After the surrender of Rotterdam, the *Leibstandarte* set out to capture The Hague, which they achieved on 15 May, capturing 3,500 Dutch prisoners of war.

Fighting in an urban landscape was particularly stressful and costly. The buildings damaged or otherwise afforded the defender the advantage. With the upper storeys of buildings available to snipers and machine gunners the attacking Waffen-SS had to think in three-dimensions and consequently expend greater amounts of ammunition and manpower in urban battles.

The tactical unit of the Waffen-SS was the ten-man squad, which comprised a squad leader and his deputy, a four-man rifle group and a machine gun group. The four-man machine gun group operated two MG 34s and provided the bulk of the squad's firepower both in offence and defence. The squad generally employed the machine gun elements to provide suppressive fire while the rifle element advanced to neutralise the enemy with grenades and rifle fire. The most common role of the rifle group was therefore to support and protect the machine gun group. The rifle element also functioned as an assault group on the attack where they were charged with taking and holding ground.

On 14 May the SS-VT Division found itself pitched against French forces for the first time. The *Panzerjager* detachment of SS *Deutchsland* soon distinguished itself knocking out five Renault tanks and a number of armoured cars.

Dutch resistance lasted until 15 May but French forces and English forces continued to resist the German forces in Holland and Northern Belgium. The SS-VT was involved in heavy fighting against French forces around Achterbroek. Fighting continued on Walcheren Island until 18 May.

On 21 May elements of the SS-VT Division were involved in the Battle of Arras against the British 5th Division, which attacked the German invaders with a strong force including around seventy tanks. It was a close run thing and the SS-VT Division suffered twenty dead and thirty wounded in the course of the morning.

On 24 May British forces attacked Saint Venant, forcing the SS-VT Division to retreat. This was a significant event as it marked the first time any SS unit had been forced to withdraw and surrender ground that it had captured to the enemy. However, the advance was soon resumed and on 27 May *Deutschland* reached a river line at Merville.

On 27 May elements of the SS-VT formed a bridgehead across the river and waited for the detached *Panzerjager* platoon SS *Totenkopf* Division to arrive and provide support and cover their exposed flank. However, the men of the *Deutschland* regiment were surprised by a unit of British tanks unexpectedly advanced on their positions. The SS-VT just managed to hold out against the British tank force, which penetrated to within fifteen feet of German positions. The day was rescued by the arrival of the *Totenkopf Panzerjager* platoon, which saved the *Deutschland* from what seemed like certain destruction.

On the night of 23 May the SS-VT had to contend with a strong breakthrough by a large French force supported by tanks. In a fierce night battle three French tanks were knocked out in the streets of the town by members of the *Germania* motorcycle infantry company.

During the closing battles with the British expeditionary force, the SS-VT enjoyed the welcome support of the 8th Panzer Division which fought on the left flank of SS *Der Führer* and was much needed given the large armoured contingents available to the French and British forces.

The British Armour continued to pose problems for the Germans who needed to allow the heavier British tanks to close to suicidally short distances in order for the puny 37 mm PAK to penetrate the frontal armour of the British armoured vehicles.

After the Dutch surrender, the *Leibstandarte* moved south to France on 24 May where they became part of the XIX Panzer Corps under the command of General Heinz Guderian. The *Leibstandarte* took up a position fifteen miles south west of Dunkirk along the line of the Aa canal, with a bridgehead established at Saint Venant. That night the OKW issued an order that the advance was to be halted despite the fact that the British Expeditionary Force was trapped.

The *Leibstandarte* paused for the night of 24 May as ordered. On the following day however, in defiance of Hitler's orders, the *Leibstandarte* continued the advance. Dietrich ordered the LAH's third battalion to cross the canal and capture the heights beyond, where British artillery observers were directing highly accurate artillery fire, which was causing heavy casualties. The third battalion assaulted the heights and overran the British positions. After the fall of France, despite his act of insubordination, Dietrich was awarded the Knight's Cross of the Iron Cross by a delighted Adolf Hitler.

The 27 of May was a black day in the history of the Waffen-SS when a unit from the *Totenkopf* (the 14th Company) was involved in the Le Paradis massacre, in which ninety-nine unarmed men of the 2nd Battalion, Royal Norfolk Regiment were machine gunned, the survivors were killed with bayonets.

By 28 May the *Leibstandarte* had taken Wormhoudt only ten miles from Dunkirk. Unfortunately, the reputation of the Waffen-SS was stained by a further atrocity which occurred here and has become known to an unforgiving posterity as the Wormhoudt massacre when the second battalion of the *Leibstandarte* killed eighty British prisoners of war in cold blood.

Dive bomber support was a key element in the early campaigns of the war. In France, the *Luftwaffe* was still in a position to operate with relative impunity and provided vital interventions.

Elements of the SS-VT were engaged in attacking the remaining French forces in the battles for Hazerouk, Cassel, Baliieul and Poperinghe, which raged from 27 to 31 May.

Between 27 and 29 May the SS-VT were also engaged in the fierce battles to dislodge the British forces from the Nieppe forest where the terrain was highly favourable to the defenders. German casualties were again high.

Following the battles of Artois and Flanders, which saw collapse of the Belgians and the withdrawal of the British, the new operation to destroy all remaining allied forces in France was launched; it was codenamed *Fall Rot* (Operation Red).

By the 4 June 1940, the bulk of the British Expeditionary Force had been forced to withdraw from Dunkirk. However, even with the British now out of the picture, there was nonetheless still plenty of hard fighting to come against the remaining French armies which were still intact and determined to defend their homeland.

On 1 June 1940, the SS-VT Division was attached to Group Von Kleist and enjoyed a brief period for rest and regrouping. It is a sobering indication of just how tough the fighting had been that the SS-VT Division, which had been in action for a little less than three weeks required 2,020 replacements. These men were fed in to the division from replacement units and incorporated into the ranks.

On June 4 the first SS-VT forces were committed to the *Fall Rot* operation which began with an artillery duel near Peronne and cost the SS Artillery regiment two killed and seventeen wounded.

On 6 June the advanced guard of *Germania* were involved in fighting on the old first world war battlefields of the Somme. The troopers observed that many trenches were still recognisable.

The Division continued south and on 7 June *Der Führer* made contact with French forces at Roye when the SS *Aufklärungsabteilung* captured two retreating field guns and two hundred French prisoners.

Advance elements of *Der Führer* met an Algerian force in company strength, which was almost entirely wiped out in a fierce firefight, which took place just outside Bouchoir.

Bouchoir was turned into a strong point for French resistance. The retreating French forces army managed to briefly re-establish some equilibrium and mounted a surprisingly strong defence which took the SS-VT by surprise and resulted in unexpectedly heavy casualties.

"In confronting the Belgian-Franco-British army's attempts to break out of its encirclement, which drew the bulk of the division into the Nieppe Forest, we demonstrated our superiority even against the stubbornly combative British forces. The battle of the Nieppe forest against an unyielding defence supported by tanks, is now a page of honour in the young history of the Regiments *Der Führer*, *Germania* and the Waffen-SS Reconnaissance Battalion."

Hausser, SS *Gruppenführer*, Division Order of the day, 3 June 1940.

The French air force remained surprisingly active well into the campaign and on the night of 8 June the advance elements of SS-VT in the Weygand line were subjected to extensive night bombing near Montdidier.

On 7 June nine armoured cars of the *Aufklärungsabteilung* advancing from Bouchoir were involved in heavy fighting outside Le Quesnel with well dug in French forces equipped with armour piercing weapons. One eight wheel armoured car was lost and its crew wounded before the force could withdraw. The other vehicles all suffered significant battle damage.

At dusk on 8 June the *Der Führer* Regiment was strongly assaulted by a regiment of the French Foreign Legion, which was found to comprise both French and German units. The attack was broken up by artillery fire from the SS Artillery Regiment.

On 8 June a fierce artillery duel took place between the SS Artillery regiment and a French battery stationed around Marquevilliers, which resulted in the destruction of the French battery.

On 12 June Kleist's Panzer group received reinforcement in the form of the SS *Liebstandarte* and also the remaining elements of the SS *Totenkopf* Division which had been held in reserve. All three Waffen-SS formations fighting in France were now to be found in the same formation.

On 9 June the SS-VT Division was involved in heavy fighting on the banks of the river Avre which required additional support from the Stukas of the *Luftwaffe* to break French resistance. The Division suffered 24 killed and 113 wounded between 6 and 9 June.

The crumbling French forces were to be allowed no time to rest and regroup. A new directive issued on 14 June by Hitler stressed the need for 'sharp pursuit' of the French in order to prevent the possibility of their forming a new front south of Paris.

On 17 June the SS-VT Division found itself involved in aggressive combat operations centred on Troyes as the three regiments of the SS-VT Division made a successful attempt to disrupt and capture retreating French forces.

The last heavy resistance encountered by SS-VT troops took place on 17 June in the heavily forested area north of Carillon where the fighting was centred on the village of Molsemes. From that point onwards, although there were still a number of combat actions, the SS-VT Division was essentially involved in seizing ground and mopping up prisoners.

Between 19 and 25 June a series of rapid advances by elements of the SS-VT led by the SS *Aufklärangsabteilung* succeeded in capturing large numbers of the French forces retreating to the southeast.

On 22 June the last combat effective French army still in the field was encircled and 500,000 men marched into captivity. The campaign in France was effectively over.

The order to cease-fire came at 01:35 hours on 25 June 1940. The battle for France was finally over. For the SS-VT there was still work to do as the battalion was tasked with occupying southwest France to the Spanish border.

Chapter Two

The Waffen-SS in the East 1941-1943

The Waffen-SS combat record in the East fashioned a reputation as an elite fighting force. However, the reputation of the Waffen-SS, the armed political wing of the *Schutzstaffel* or Nazi party, will always be tainted by the war crimes they committed in the East including the killing of what the Nazis termed *untermenschen* or sub humans – Slavs, Jews and Marxists.

In a speech Hitler gave to Waffen-SS troops just three weeks before the start of Operation Barbarossa he espoused their joint philosophy: "This is an ideological battle and a struggle of races. Here stands a world as we conceived it – beautiful, decent, socially equal and full of culture; this is what our Germany is like. On the other side stands a population of 180,000,000, a mixture of races, whose very names are unpronounceable and whose physique is such that one can only shoot them down without mercy or compassion. When you fight over there in the east, you are carrying on the same struggle against the same sub-humanity, the same inferior races, that at one time appeared under the name of Huns, another time of Magyars, another time of Tartars, and still another time under the name of Genghis Khan and the Mongols. Today they appear as Russians under the political banner of Bolshevism."

When he launched Operation Barbarossa Hitler expected the *Wehrmacht* to conquer the Soviet Union and the Waffen-SS to Nazify it. It was the biggest invasion in the history of human conflict. On one side were over three million well trained, equipped and battle hardened German troops including the Waffen-SS and half a million of their Axis allies. In total the Germans had 153 divisions including 21 Panzer and 14 motorised divisions containing over 3,400 tanks and 3,000 aircraft. On the other side was a Soviet army of over five million men in 180 divisions with over 10,000 tanks and 20,000 aircraft. However, while on paper the Soviets seemed more than a match for the Germans, in reality their troops were badly organised and ill equipped and many of their tanks and aircraft were obsolete. Most importantly the Soviet army had lost many of its best commanders due to Stalin's purges.

To the *Wehrmacht* Hitler ordered the job of "kicking in the front door so the whole rotten Russian edifice will come tumbling down". To the Waffen-SS fell not just the job of combat but also waging a race war to create Hitler's long cherished dream of *lebensraum* or living space for the German people in the East, a theory first mooted in his 1926 political testimony, *'Mein Kampf'*. Barbarossa was therefore always more than just a military campaign, it was a battle of ideologies between National Socialism and Communism to establish a new world order in Europe.

During operations in the east the Waffen-SS grew rapidly from just six divisions comprising 160,000 men at the start of Barbarossa until, by the end of the war, it was a huge force of 38 combat divisions comprising over 950,000 men. Distinctive uniforms, strict Germanic racial requirements and patronage under the wing of two leading Nazi benefactors, Heinrich Himmler, one of the post powerful men in the Third Reich, and, of course, the Führer himself, marked the Waffen-SS as a favoured formation. As a consequence they attracted only the most committed recruits who were willing to fight and die for the cause. Nonetheless, its combat reputation had to be forged in battle and the Waffen-SS soon earned a fearsome reputation as a hard fighting combat force.

In the East, Waffen-SS divisions were placed under the operational control of the *Oberkommando des Heeres* or the Supreme High Command of the Army although in practice they often acted independently. While initially numerically insignificant when compared to the *Heer* or the Germany Army, the Waffen-SS soon brought to Barbarossa an ideological fanaticism out of all proportion to their numbers.

For the over stretched German Army, with its history steeped in the old Imperial and Prussian traditions of solidarity and soldiering, indulging in any activities like racial cleansing which did not progress their war aims was regarded as a waste of resources. For the Waffen-SS the regular army lacked the ideological zeal and fighting spirit to beat an opponent who would often rather die than be captured. The result was a severely strained relationship between the two who often disagreed on tactical issues.

The sense of racial and military superiority, encouraged by Himmler through better pay, food and equipment, was central to the Waffen-SS philosophy. That philosophy was combined with a fanatical loyalty to Hilter, best expressed in the motto *"Meine Ehre heisst Treue"* or "My honour is loyalty". It meant that at the start of Barbarossa the divisions which comprised the Waffen-SS, the SS *Leibstandarte Adolf Hitler*, SS *Das Reich*, SS *Totenkopf*, SS *Polizei* and SS *Nord* were all recruited from the toughest and most ideological ethnic Germans. The exception was the SS *Wiking* Division which was built from SS-VT *Germania* as featured in Chapter 1 of this book. They recruited initially from Scandinavian, Finnish, Estonian, Dutch and Belgian volunteers but all served under German officers.

The *Wehrmacht* launched its surprise attack on Russia at 3.15 a.m. on 22 June 1941, bombing positions in Soviet occupied Poland. Attached to the three huge army groups were the six Waffen-SS divisions. Army Group North advanced through the Baltic States and on to Leningrad, accompanied by SS *Totenkopf*, SS *Polizei* and SS *Nord*. Army Group Centre including SS *Das Reich* headed towards Moscow with the SS *Leibstandarte* and SS *Wiking* were with Army Group South and marched towards the Ukraine and Kiev.

During the first six months of Barbarossa the sheer scale of the Soviet rout in the East surprised even the German generals. On the opening day alone the *Luftwaffe* destroyed over 2,000 Soviet aircraft, many on the ground and Army Group North penetrated over 50 miles into Russian territory. By the end of the first week Army Group Centre had captured Minsk and by the end of June they had advanced over 200 miles towards Moscow. By the end of September Army Group South had captured nearly half a million Soviet troops during the Battle of Kiev and Army Group North had lay siege to Leningrad. At the spearhead of all these successful advances in the East was the Waffen-SS.

Yet just three months later on 1 December 1941 inside the outskirts of Moscow the offensive ground to a shuddering halt in temperatures of minus 40 Fahrenheit. Five days later the Red Army counter attacked driving the Germans back 40 miles. During Operation Typhoon or the attack on Moscow SS *Das Reich* suffered big losses and of the 2,000 grenadiers who had started out with the regiment that June only 35 were left alive by the end of December. However, this crushing defeat for Germany was to prove the making of the Waffen-SS.

By the end of 1941 the Waffen-SS had suffered over 43,000 casualties across the Eastern Front. One in four troops had either been killed or wounded. However, it was widely recognised even by the *Wehrmacht* that they had fought with great tenacity and without them the German army would not have got to the gates of Moscow. Eberhard von Macksensen, commander of III Army Corps in Army Group South, writing to Himmler said the SS *Leibstandarte* had demonstrated "inner discipline, cool daredevilry, cheerful enterprise, unshakeable firmness in a crisis, exemplary toughness and camaraderie". The legend of the fanatical fighting spirit of the Waffen-SS had been born.

By the beginning of 1942 the Soviet Union was bloodied but unbowed. The changing fortunes of the campaign were exposed in February 1942 by the encirclement of 100,000 Germans troops from Army Group North in the Demyansk pocket, south of Leningrad. The forces included the SS Division *Totenkopf* who were again at the forefront of the fighting. It was this division which led the breakout in April 1941. However, they paid a high price with 15,000 troops either killed or wounded. After this the Waffen-SS were never again to regain the initiative in the East but were to fight with distinction at Kharkov and Kursk.

Operation Barbarossa was the German codename for the attack on Russia. The attack commenced at 3.15 a.m. on 22 June 1941. Over 3 million German troops and half a million of its allies attacked across an 1,800 mile front in three massive army groups. The *Wehrmacht* was accompanied by six Waffen-SS Divisions.

Army Group North advanced through the Baltic States and on to Leningrad, it contained three Waffen-SS Divisions; *Totenkopf*, *Polizei* and *Nord*. Army Group Centre headed to Moscow with *Das Reich*. *Leibstandarte* and *Wiking* were with Army Group South and drove towards Ukraine and Kiev.

Motorcycles of the *Wiking* Division scout ahead of the Panzers. The speed and ferocity of the German attack caught the Russians completely by surprise.

A 7.5 cm *leichtes Infanteriegeschütz* 18 or 7.5 cm le.IG 18, infantry support gun is brought up to support the troops. It had a rate of fire of 8-12 rounds per minute and a range of 3,550 metres. The crew put their fingers in their ears to reduce the noise.

An SS *Totenkopf Panzerabwehrkanone* 36 or 3.7 cm anti tank gun is towed towards the front, 1941. It proved of little use against the Russian T-34 tank so acquired the nickname *Heeresanklopfgerät*, or *'tank door knocker'*. It was replaced a year later by the more powerful 5 cm Pak 38.

The 6th Panzer Division *Das Nord* fought with Army Group North and saw action right up to the Arctic Circle. Here they have brought up a 7.5 cm *leichtes Infanteriegeschütz* 18 or 7.5 cm le.IG 18 infantry support gun to fire on partisans hiding in the woods and marshes of Karelia.

Totenkopf troops leave behind a burning Russian village in the opening weeks of Barbarossa. The division was notorious for its ethnic cleansing. It's Death's Head insignia reflected the fact that many early recruits were concentration camp guards.

Note the swastika on the side car of this *Totenkopf* motorcycle, used for recognition by the *Luftwaffe*. The autumn rains turned many roads into quagmires, and in turn, the Germans lost many vehicles.

Waffen-SS troops storm a village during Operation Barbarossa. The Germans were surprised that the Soviets vigorously defended even quite small villages.

Huge demands were made on the infantry who had to march vast distances of up to 40 miles a day in order to keep up with the fast moving Panzers.

The wing of a crashed Soviet aircraft makes a sign-post for the troops following in the wake of the rapidly advancing reconnaissance section.

Grenadiers advance behind two Waffen-SS *Das Reich Sonderkraftfahrzeug 251* or Sd.Kfz251 half-tracks. It was the largest and best armoured German half-track and was designed to take the *Panzergrenadiers* or the motorised infantry into battle.

A 20 mm Flak 30 anti aircraft gun is brought up to support the attack. Although designed as an anti aircraft gun it was also extensively used as an infantry support gun. It was the most numerous German artillery gun produced during the war.

A Waffen-SS soldier with an MG 42 machine gun. Robust and reliable, it was capable of firing over 1,000 rounds a minute.

An SS Grenadier proudly displays his, *Eisernes Kreuz 2 Klasse* or Iron Cross 2nd Class for bravery on the battlefield, 1941. Over 4.5 million Iron Crosses were awarded in World War Two.

Totenkopf troops crossing a makeshift bridge in a Horsh 108 troop carrier. Note the Death's Head insignia on the rear.

The Reconnaissance Battalion of the SS *Wiking* Division scout ahead of the infantry and tanks. *Wiking* Division was recruited from Scandinavian, Finnish, Estonian, Dutch and Belgian volunteers but served under German officers.

Waffen-SS troops using an anti tank gun against the Soviet T-34 tank. The T-34 was heavily armoured and it required a direct hit to its tracks or at very close range to disable it.

A Waffen-SS soldier from *Leibstandarte* Division watches a village burn. As the campaign progressed many Soviet fighters rather than surrender went into hiding and formed partisan units who operated behind German lines.

Soldiers from the *Wiking* Division use a flamethrower against Soviet troops. This Model 35 flamethrower had a capacity of 2.5 gallons and a range of 25 yards. They were operated by engineers rather than combat troops and were most effective at close range against pillboxes.

Waffen-SS *Funker* or radio operator receives a message for his unit. The attack on Russia posed a serious challenge in terms of communication because of the speed of the advance and the great distances involved along the fronts.

Das Reich troops cross a river after the Soviets had blown up the bridge. The Germans attack depended upon Panzer engineers being able to quickly establish temporary pontoon bridges capable of supporting tanks.

Waffen-SS troops firing an MG 42 machine gun. It was the standard machine gun from 1942 onwards replacing the MG 34 and had one of the highest rates of fire of any single barrelled gun at 1,200–1,500 rounds per minute.

Waffen-SS troops man a machine gun post covering the approach road to Louhi, 1941. In 1941 the German advance was so swift that they would encircle whole Russian armies who would then become trapped miles behind the front line.

An *SS* radio operator receives their next orders. Good communication between the Panzer tanks and the infantry following them ensured that in the opening months of Barbarossa the Germans retained tactical surprise.

The Russian winter took a very heavy toll on the Germans who unlike the Soviets were not equipped with winter clothing. By November 1941, the Germans had suffered 730,000 casualties.

Waffen-SS troops put together a "Panzer cocktail", an improvised Molotov cocktail used against the Russian T-34 tank. Due to its sloping armour the 3.7 cm anti-tank gun proved ineffective against it.

The SS Calvalry Brigade in 1941. It was mainly involved in anti-partisan operations. In 1942 it was upgraded into 8th SS Cavalry Division or *Florian Geyer*.

The Russian winter of 1941 came early and by November it had begun to seriously affect the morale of German troops. The Soviet counteroffensives launched in December further exhausted and demoralized the German troops.

Das Reich, part of Army Group Centre, reached the gates of Moscow in December 1941 but the weather, massive losses and a Soviet counteroffensive forced the division back.

The 4th SS *Polizei* Division advances on Leningrad. The siege of Leningrad started on 8 September 1941 and was not lifted until 27 January 1944. At 372 days long it was one of the longest and most costly sieges in history.

Waffen-SS snipers on the Eastern Front. He is equipped with the standard German army rifle the Karbiner 98k Kurz with a telescopic sight. Rifles which were exceptionally accurate in factory tests were specifically allocated to snipers for this task. They had an effective range of 1,000 metres.

A 3.7 cm anti-tank gun is towed along on runners by horses. The gun while an effective infantry support weapon proved ineffective against Russian tanks like the T-34 and KV 1 and 2.

The Waffen-SS use high explosives and mines to blow up dams of ice blocking a river. The Germans also used mines against the Soviet T-34 tank. With its thick sloping armour the Germans found the Russian tank a formidable opponent.

The hardest winter in 120 years, a record temperature of over minus 40 degrees Fahrenheit was recorded in December 1941. The Germans were not trained or equipped to fight in such conditions.

Waffen-SS troops with an MG 34 heavy machine gun. The legs could be extended to allow it to be used as an anti-aircraft gun or lowered so it could be used as an infantry support weapon.

An abandoned *Wiking* motorcycle and sidecar. The spring and autumn rains in Russia were known as the 'mud season' and claimed many valuable vehicles severely hampering the German war effort.

Waffen-SS engineers help build a road. Although making sure that roads were passable was the job of engineers, in practice it was a preoccupation of all soldiers because it was such a mammoth task.

Troops from *Das Reich* Division rest on the outskirts of Moscow, December 1941. The division was decimated by the Soviet counter offensive and was withdrawn for rest and refitting.

From their positions west of Moscow soldiers in *Das Reich* could clearly see the Soviet capital through their binoculars. It was the closest they would ever get. The German army would never again threaten the Russian capital.

SS *Wiking* Division soldiers hitch a lift on a Panzer III tank, 1942. Due to continuing losses at the hands of the Russian T-34 tank a year later the Panzer III was superseded by the Panzer IV and the Panther.

Waffen-SS troops in Yugoslavia. It was overrun by Germans forces just before the start of Operation Barbarossa in what became known as the 'April War' and Waffen-SS units continued to operate there throughout the campaign in the East. Invading Yugoslavia delayed the onset of the attack on Russia. Throughout Operation Barbarossa partisans kept valuable Waffen-SS units pinned down and away from the Eastern Front.

A Waffen-SS anti aircraft gun protects a bridge being built by Waffen-SS engineers. Although thousands of Soviet planes were destroyed during the opening months of Barbarossa, the Soviet air force regained the initiative in 1942 and became a far greater threat to the attacking Germans.

Waffen-SS troops got better food and more rations than *Wehrmacht* troops which further strained the relationship. Napoleon's quote that an army marches on its stomach was especially true on the Eastern Front and the more generous rations the Waffen-SS received were vital in maintaining morale.

Waffen-SS troops sort through the *feldpost* or field post. The Waffen-SS had their own post and officers made sure that the post got through to the front line whatever the conditions, mindful of how important it was to morale.

Waffen-SS troops on their way to the Balkans. Partisan activity in the Balkans pinned down many Waffen-SS units and kept them from reinforcing their comrades on the Eastern Front.

Reconnaissance attached to the Waffen-SS played a vital part in the German advance and later the retreat from Russia, pinpointing enemy positions and searching for cover. Reconnaissance units were responsible for scouting ahead as SS Divisions were often in the vanguard of the fighting in Russia. The soldier, top, is using a scissors periscope.

Waffen-SS troops inspect an unexploded rocket. The Soviet Katyusha rocket launcher took a heavy toll of both German troops and equipment. Compared to other artillery, multiple rocket launchers could deliver a devastating amount of explosives to a target area quickly. However, they had lower accuracy and required a longer time to reload than conventional artillery.

Waffen-SS forces advance as part of Operation Blue in 1942. Over-stretched by the vast area they had overrun, German forces would go on to fight an epic battle at Stalingrad which resulted in the destruction of the Sixth Army.

Exhausted and demoralised Waffen-SS troops ride on a *Sonderkraftfahrzeug* or Sd.Kfz10, a special motorised vehicle, late 1942. The autumn rains again slowed the advance, putting great strain on both men and machines.

Waffen-SS soldiers line up before a captured Russian T-34 tank. The T-34 inflicted huge losses on the attacking Germans due to its firepower, armour, speed and reliability.

A wounded soldier from the 4th SS Division *Polizei*. The division was officially formed in 1942 from its origins as a German police organisation. They took part in heavy fighting between January and March which resulted in the destruction of the Soviet 2nd Shock Army.

Outclassed by the Russian T-34 and KV tanks and difficult to repair, the Panzer III was nevertheless the core of the German mechanised divisions and over 5,700 were built.

An SS radio operator receives their next orders. Good communication between the Panzer tanks and the infantry was what made the German war machine so successful.

A Flak 30 or 20 mm anti-aircraft gun in action. A lightweight gun, it was easy to transport but its low fire power of only 120 rounds a minute let it down.

Waffen-SS troops cross a river on the Atlantic coast in August 1942. Waffen-SS divisions were withdrawn from the fierce fighting on the Eastern Front to recuperate and be refitted in the West.

A curious Waffen-SS grenadier inspects the interior of a knocked out T-34. The numerous hits confirm that the T-34 menace could be defeated by a combination of steadfast gunnery and steely resolve.

The crew of a tank bivouacking in the field. Any period of rest, however brief, provided a well earned rest from the constant advance.

Waffen-SS troops watch the battle from their *Sonderkraftfahrzeug* 251 or Sd.Kfz 251 armoured fighting vehicle built by the Hanomag company. Heavily armoured it was a versatile vehicle which was well liked by the troops and known simply as a *"Hanomag"* by both German and Allied soldiers.

Waffen-SS troops prepare to attack. They were better equipped than the *Wehrmacht* and despite accounting for only a small proportion of the total number of German troops involved in the East, often formed the spearhead of the attack.

A grenadier from the 8th SS Calvary Panzer Division *Florian Geyer* holds an anti-tank "Teller" mine to use against a Russian T-34 tank. Shaped like a plate and packed with 5.5 kilograms of high explosive with a detonation pressure of about 200 pounds, the teller mine was capable of blowing the tracks off any Soviet tank.

Chapter Three

The Waffen-SS in Combat 1943-1945

From 1943 to 1945 the Waffen-SS, in the East were engaged in a long and bloody retreat against a numerically far superior enemy. As they fell back across the vast plains of the Soviet Union, Poland, Hungary and ultimately Germany itself, death or ignominious defeat at the hands of the Red Army became their fate. But the Waffen-SS, true to their character, fought a fanatical rearguard action to the end. In the process they showed utterly heroic if increasingly futile acts of bravery against overwhelming odds.

In the west too the SS had an unenviable task of attempting to hold back superior allied forces. Nonetheless, many SS formations fought with distinction and it was SS divisions SS *Hohenstaufen* and SS *Frundsberg* fighting together as *II Panzer Korps* who won the distinction of having engineered the victory at Arnhem which was the last clear cut triumph for German arms in World War II.

The devastating defeat at Stalingrad in February 1943 epitomised the changing fortunes of the Germany army or *Wehrmacht* in the East. To counter what he saw as the defeatist attitude of the army, Hitler increasingly turned to the Waffen-SS whose loyalty and fighting spirit were never in question. The *Wehrmacht's* loss became the burden of the Waffen-SS as the *Führer's* 'fire brigade' were used to plug the gaps and hold the line against the marauding Red Army.

Hitler's confidence in the abilities of the SS to produce results against the odds were underlined in March 1943 when the SS Panzer Corps, under the charismatic leadership of Paul 'Papa' Hausser, nicknamed the father of the Waffen-SS, pulled off a spectacular victory at Kharkov temporarily halting the Soviet advance. The pictures in this book bear witness to the military skills and initiative those men showed in the face of an overwhelming enemy.

However Hausser's Panzer Corps had found themselves trapped in the city and with the defeat at Stalingrad still a fresh memory Hitler ordered them to "stand fast and fight to the death". Risking Hitler's wrath Hausser ignored him and instead sanctioned a strategic withdraw to prevent his tanks being decimated in the besieged city. In response Hitler flew into a blind rage and tried to sack his wayward commander. However, Hausser regrouped and without *Luftwaffe* support made a direct attack on Kharkov, eventually recapturing it after four days of intensive, house to house fighting. For his bravery Hausser was awarded the Oak Leaves to his Knights Cross and officially pardoned.

However, it was to be the last victory for the Waffen-SS in the East. The offensive resulted in the Red Army suffering over 70,000 casualties but in an ominous sign of the battles to come the SS Panzer Corps lost nearly half its strength.

Ironically the success of the Third Battle of Kharkov was to prove a turning point in the East not for Hitler but for Stalin because it lulled the Germans back into a false sense of their own superiority. Reinvigorated by the victory, in July 1943 Hitler sought to eliminate the Kursk salient, a bulge where the Soviet advance jutted westwards for about 80 miles into the German line. The result was Operation Citadel, the largest tank battle in history. It pitched 900,000 Germans with 2,700 tanks and 2,000 aircraft against some 1.3 million Russians with 3,600 tanks and 2,400 aircraft. Once again the Waffen-SS were in the forefront of the fighting.

The remains of the Waffen-SS in the East now found themselves constantly on the retreat. On 25 August Kharkov once again fell to the Soviets, this time for good. By the beginning of September the Germans had suffered over half a million casualties in fifty days and 1,600 tanks and assault guns had been destroyed or knocked out. Soviet casualties are not known but historians estimate them at twice the number of German ones. But for Hitler the losses were unsustainable and the Battle of Kursk proved to be the last German offensive in the East. Alexander Kovalenko, a Soviet pilot, flying over a battlefield littered with German armour declared triumphantly "The enemy's front is broken. We are advancing."

After Kursk morale in the army began to disintegrate but in the Waffen-SS a fanatical, if increasingly futile, fighting spirit lived on. Panzer officer Tassilo von Bogenhardt was typical and said after the battle "Each German soldier considered himself superior to any single Russian, even though their numbers were so overpowering. The slow, orderly retreat did not depress us too much. We felt we were holding our own." His illusion was rudely shattered shortly afterwards when he was badly wounded and then captured by the Soviets, the worst fate that could befall a Waffen-SS soldier.

By the end of 1943 half the territory taken by the Germans since 1941 was back under Soviet control. Russia had lost over twenty million men or nearly eighty per cent of its total war casualties. But they were no longer on their own. The Allies had successfully invaded Italy and six months later on 6 June 1944 came the D-Day landings. For the Waffen-SS this meant fighting on two fronts and more divisions being diverted from the East to the West, further weakening their ability to defend the 'Fatherland against Bolshevism'.

Even in retreat, however, the Waffen-SS proved themselves to be a formidable fighting unit. By 1945 under the operational command of Heinrich Himmler, the Waffen-SS had expanded to 38 divisions many of whom were conscripts. This army within an army amounted to over 900,000 men. As the situation in the East deteriorated they were drawn from an ever more diverse ethnic mix such as the 13th Waffen-SS *Handschar* Division which was composed of Bosnian Muslims and conducted anti partisan activities in Yugoslavia and Croatia in 1944. The result was that by the finish of the Second World

War nearly half of the Waffen-SS were non German nationals despite the original strict racial requirements laid down by Himmler.

As the war in the East moved to Poland and eventually Germany, Waffen-SS troops were among the final soldiers defending the ruins of the Reich Chancellery in Berlin as Hitler committed suicide on 30 April 1945. When news of his death reached them, many of the remaining Waffen-SS troops shot themselves rather than surrender to the Soviets.

After hostilities had finally ceased on 8 May 1945 nearly one in three Waffen-SS troops were dead or missing in action. For an elite fighting force which never made up more than 10 per cent of the total German Army and had numbered just 120 men in 1933, they had fought with almost reckless courage and paid a very high price. Their mortality rate was the equivalent of all the casualties suffered by the United States military during the entire war.

The Waffen-SS had been overwhelmed by an enemy simply too strong in men and material. However, as their military situation had worsened so had their atrocities while non-combat SS units were directly culpable when it came to the worst atrocities. Praise for the Waffen-SS as a fighting force needs to be balanced against their inhuman political philosophy and the utter ruthlessness they frequently demonstrated particularly towards the Jews, Soviets and later the Poles in the suppression of the Warsaw uprising in 1944 where the name of Otto Dirlewanger will forever live on in infamy. Accordingly history has judged the Waffen-SS not as they would have wished by their combat record but instead far more ignominiously by the record of the monstrous regime which spawned them. When serious historians review the campaign in the East the fighting record of the Waffen-SS is rightly seen in the context of Hitler's ideological war against the Soviet Union. As a result there is an indelible stain on their combat record and after the war many Waffen-SS veterans were deprived of pension rights. While some were involved in atrocities, others fought honourably given the fog of war which afflicted both sides. As these pictures show many Waffen-SS troops distinguished themselves in combat and showed incredible bravery, often against overwhelming odds.

War crimes aside, the military esteem the Waffen-SS were held in can perhaps best be judged not by their rivals in the *Wehrmacht* but by their hated adversaries in the Red Army. At the victory parade in Red Square in Moscow on 24 June 1945, pride of place among the captured Nazi standards went to the first Waffen-SS division, the *Leibstandarte Adolf Hitler*.

Panzers are massed for a concentrated attack during 'Operation Citadel' or the Battle of Kursk.

The Battle of Kursk pitched 900,000 Germans with 2,700 tanks and 2,000 aircraft against some 1.3 million Russians with 3,600 tanks and 2,400 aircraft.

Tiger tanks advance during the Battle of Kursk. Although superior in fire power and armour to the Soviet T-34, the Germans had too few of them.

Inside a Tiger tank: the driver (above), and the radio operator (below).

When introduced in August 1942 it was the most powerful tank in the world and continued to cause both military and psychological fear in the Soviets until the end of the war.

Inside a Tiger tank: the gunner (above), and the commander (below).

With its highly accurate 88 mm gun the Tiger was feared by the Soviets but was over engineered, expensive to produce and difficult to repair. As a result only 1,300 were made during the whole war.

A Panther and a half-track move across the Russian steppes in 1943. The Kursk offensive in the summer of 1943, failed to re-set the balance of power of the Eastern Front.

Waffen-SS in the trenches during the Battle of Kursk, July 1943. The trooper in the foreground wears a beard, a rather uncommon liberty in the SS allowed to some foreign volunteers.

Operation Citadel begins. The German plan was to cut off the Kursk salient by making two pincer attacks at its neck. Infantrymen mark the forward edge of the battle line for the *Luftwaffe*.

In the opening days of the Battle of Kursk the Waffen-SS made rapid progress penetrating deep into Soviet territory.

Waffen-SS machine gunner during the second Battle of Kursk, July 1943.

Members of the Waffen-SS discuss tactics with a tank commander and then move into position. Operation Citadel was the largest tank battle in history.

Waffen-SS infantrymen advance carrying boxes of ammunition. The Kursk salient was a trap because the Soviets had got prior warning about the German offensive from the 'Lucy' spy ring in Switzerland.

As the Germans pushed forward the Soviets waited for their chance to counterattack. The faces of these young Waffen-SS infantrymen already show the exhaustion of battle.

As the Germans continued the advance they had no idea that the battle plans to eliminate the Kursk bulge had been leaked to Stalin. Despite mounting losses the Germans continued to push forward..

Sturmbannführer Hack, the commander of a *Panzergrenadier* battalion.

During the long retreat Waffen-SS units would often counterattack the advancing Russians, giving the regular army time to withdraw to more strategic lines of defence. However, they only brought temporary relief due to the sheer weight of numbers the Soviets were throwing into the advance.

A Panther tank moves forward into action.

The Panzer IV was in service until 1945. This machine is serving with the SS Panzer Division *Totenkopf*.

A mortar is being assembled prior to action.

A signaller in the process of checking the line, a relentless task.

Waffen-SS troops retreat across a river. The Soviets made full use of the natural features around Kursk to pursue and attack the Germans knowing they were vulnerable crossing water.

The retreat was slowed by the poor conditions of the Russian roads which even in summer could become impassable after a flash storm.

Towards the end of the war the hard pressed Waffen-SS Panzer divisions were rushed continuously from one sector to another..

An excellent study of a Panther moving in the open.

An MG 42 mounted on its tripod proved to be an excellent heavy machine-gun.

A 2 cm Flak cannon spotting for enemy aircraft.

Panther tanks in support positions behind a rudimentary command position.

Men of *SS-Fallschirmjäger* Battalion 500 operating a mortar in a forward position during the 1944 operation designed to eliminate Tito.

The main dressing station of the *SS-Fallschirmjäger* Battalion 500.

Estonian SS volunteers of the 20th Waffen-SS Grenadier Division in combat on the Eastern Front.

Panther tanks of the *Wiking* tank regiment played a decisive part in the successful break out from the Korsun-Tscherkassy Pocket.

The command H.Q. of the *Wiking* Division in the encircled city of Kovel.

A Sherman tank provided to the Soviets by America lies upturned and abandoned after a fall from the bridge. A Waffen-SS supply column is seen passing by the wreck.

An assault group of the *Wiking* Division moves up along a railway embankment to relieve the pocket at Kovel.

A *Maultier* half-track truck passes discarded supply canisters dropped by air. From March 20 1944 until the end of the fighting, 1,329 canisters and 22 cases were dropped into the Kovel pocket.

A command Panther tank of the *Wiking* Division lies abandoned having been knocked out during the drive to Kovel.

The Panther tanks of the *Wiking* Division were accompanied by *Panzergrenadiers* of the 2nd Company of the 5th Engineers Battalion. Both the grenadiers and tank crews suffered heavy losses.

Two more studies of the Panthers which were knocked out on the railway line approaching Kovel.

A surprisingly cheerful assembly of grenadiers are pictured during the withdrawal from the Narew triangle.

The 11th *Panzergrenadier* Division *Nordland* during the withdrawal from the Narva bridgehead. Seen in the background is a *Marder* III tank destroyer, built on the chassis of the Panzer 38(t).

A local civilian provides information on the movements of enemy units during the summer of 1944.

5th Company of the *Wiking* Panzer Regiment during a brief halt in the fighting.

SS-Obersturmführer Nicolussi-Leck, Commander of the 8th Company of SS Panzer Regiment 5, *Wiking* Division, receives the Knight's Cross.

Men of the 5th SS Panzer Division *Wiking* in combat positions.

A Dutch volunteer of the Waffen-SS carrying a roll of barbed wire during the fighting in the River Narva area.

Anti-tank mines were laid according to a strict plan, so that they could be collected and reused again if necessary.

Michael Wittmann, the legendary Commander of the 1st Company, Heavy Panzer Battalion 501, knocked out 138 tanks and so was the most successful tank soldier of the Second World War.

Balthaser Woll (right), was the gunner of Wittmann's crew during most of his combat successes. Woll was not present when Wittmann was killed on 8 June 1944.

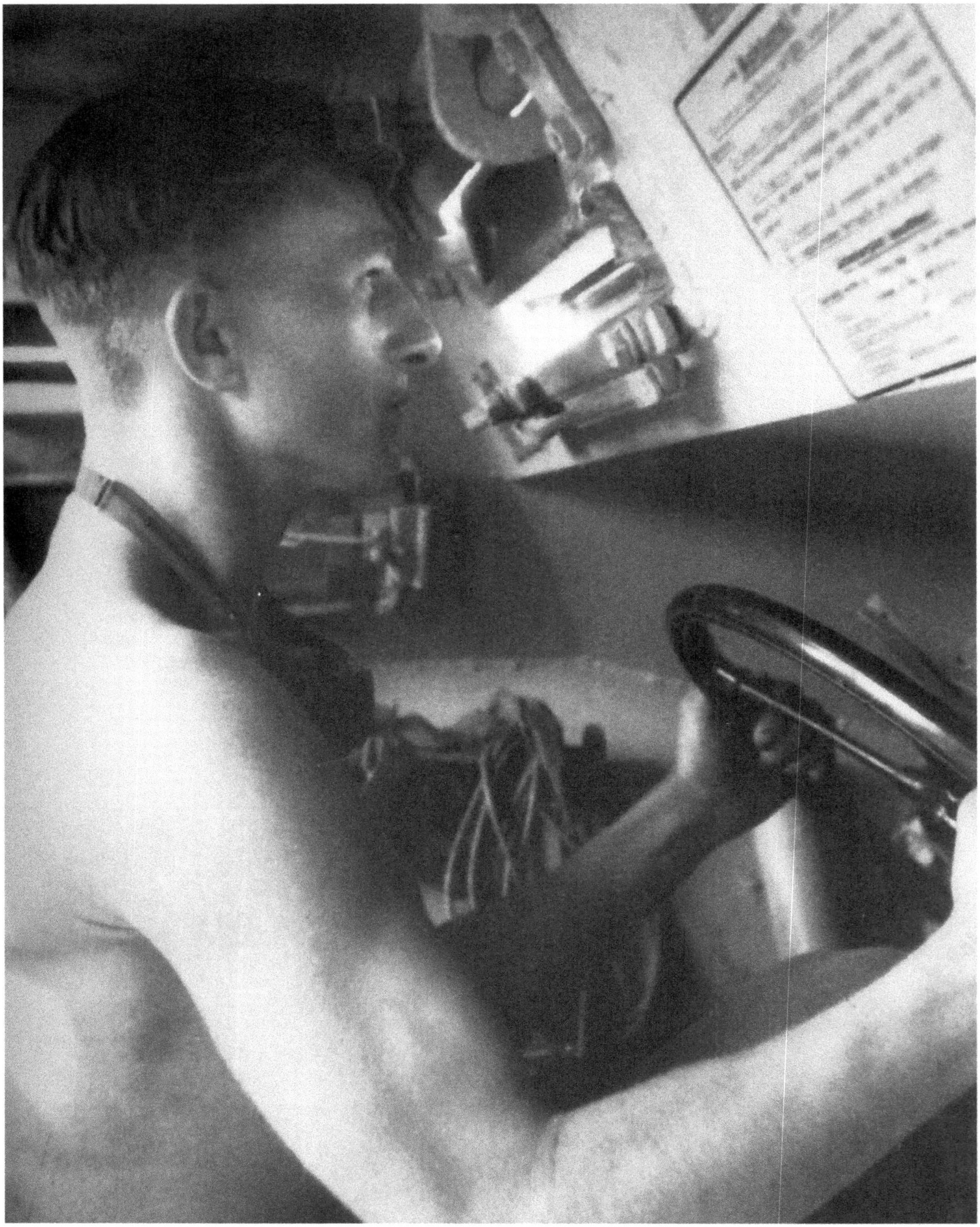

A trainee tank driver undergoing instruction.

An excellent study of the command post of a Panzer battalion which is located underneath a tank.

Waffen-SS prisoners captured during the fighting in the West. These men faced a frightening ordeal at the hands of the Western Allies. This paled into insignificance compared to the treatment meted out by the Russians.

SS *Panzergrenadiers* photographed during the fighting to the west of Caen.

Hitler Youth visit the 12th SS Panzer Division, 21 March 1944 in Belgium.

Dead German SS Grenadier; Normandy, 19 June 1944.

The strain of battle shows on the faces of these grenadiers fighting in Normandy during June 1944.

A German Grenadier equipped with the *Panzerschrek* or 'Stove Pipe'. This powerful anti-tank weapon was highly efficient at short range.

German vehicles and armour destroyed from the air by Allied fighter bombers. The vehicle in the foreground is a *Kubelwagen*, a general purpose vehicle.

SS *Obersturmführer* or Lieutenant Colonel Erwin Meier-Dress, Knights Cross, August 1944. A Panzer Ace, he was killed a year later trying to relieve the Soviet siege of Budapest.

Young SS men captured in the immediate aftermath of the Normandy landings. The average age of the SS Division *Hitlerjugend* was officially given as eighteen – in practice there were a fair number in the ranks who were much younger.

A powerful demonstration of the destructive capacity of Allied air power. This jumble of wreckage represents the vehicles of a German division which were caught by the bombs of Allied heavy bombers at Rouen Docks, as the German forces desperately tried to find a route over the Seine.

A member of the Hitler Youth Division is taken into captivity in the aftermath of the Normandy battles. Although the Hitler Youth Division fought very well in the campaign, they could not escape the inevitable end which awaited them.

A knocked out Tiger I in the ruins of Villers-Bocage.

The Tiger I that knocked out the first M26 Pershing in combat. The Tiger then backed into a rubble pile and became stuck. The crew abandoned the tank.

Allied troops sift through the wreckage of a German supply column destroyed from the air as it retreated through the Falaise gap. In the foreground are the remains of a German half-track and a motor cycle. The German armies which took to the field in Normandy included over one million men, supported by over 1,500 tanks and some 3,500 guns. This vast assemblage needed over 20,000 vehicles and 20,000 horses. By the end of the campaign, the Germans had lost some 240,000 men killed and wounded, a further 200,000 as prisoners of war and practically all of the tanks, guns and vehicles. In that respect, the battle for Normandy must rank as a strategic victory on a par with the destruction of the Army Group Centre, the outcome of Operation Bagration which was taking place in Russia, at the same time. Taken together these two campaigns represent the decisive blows from which there was no possible prospect of recovery.

An Allied Sherman passes American infantry standing amidst the wreckage of German armour. The numbered object in the foreground is the turret of a German tank, which has been completely blown off the chassis. The vehicle in the background appears to be a Tiger Mark One.

A poignant reminder of the ever-present danger of sudden death for the soldiers on both sides.

Four Waffen-SS troopers taken prisoner from 9th SS Reconnaissance Battalion at Arnhem Bridge, one is a seventeen-year-old. All of them are wearing the camouflage uniforms that were peculiar to the Waffen-SS; these are not snipers.

Bodies and wrecked material litter the narrow lanes of the German escape route in the Falaise pocket.

An *SS-Panzergrenadier* in Normandy, 21 June 1944.

Waffen-SS grenadiers aboard a *Sturmgeschütz* during the advance in the Ardennes, December 1944.

A wrecked German half-track from an SS Division lies on its side next to one of its fallen occupants. The American soldier is standing aboard a *Wespe*, one of the new breed of German self-propelled artillery which provided effective fire support for the Panzer divisions. They were, however, never available in adequate numbers; only 635 of these very useful vehicles were produced to satisfy the unceasing demands of both the Western and Eastern fronts.

An armoured SdKfz 251 half-track of the SS-Panzer Division *Das Reich* and the corpse of a German soldier near Mortain, 12 August 1944.

Waffen-SS tanks from the 3rd Division *Totenkopf* and snipers in Poland, July 1944. After the Soviets launched Operation Bagration, the largest and last offensive to be launched from Russian soil, the SS Panzer Corps were the only line of defence after the destruction of Army Group Centre.

Initially the Poles took over the city centre but savage fighting saw the Germans take back control in September 1944. 25 per cent of Warsaw buildings were destroyed and together with earlier damage over 85 per cent of the city had been razed to the ground when the Soviets entered in January 1945.

Waffen-SS troops carry a wounded comrade on a stretcher. One in three Waffen-SS troops died or went missing in action during the long retreat.

Waffen-SS troops hitch a ride on the back of a Panzer tank. From 1944 onwards they found themselves in almost constant retreat.

German troops rest behind 'snow walls' in the winter of 1944 on the Eastern front. Given the speed of the Russian offensive they were often the only defensive positions they could construct.

A reconnaissance troop makes its way to the Russian line in the northern sector of the Eastern front. Unlike the *Wehrmacht* morale among Waffen-SS remained in the main high.

The mud splattered face of defeat on a motorcycle messenger of the *Prinz Eugen* Division.

Waffen-SS troops try in vain to stem the Soviet advance. By 1944 severe shortages of winter clothing meant that they had to rely on the generosity of civilians who were asked by the Nazi regime to donate furs and other winter coats.

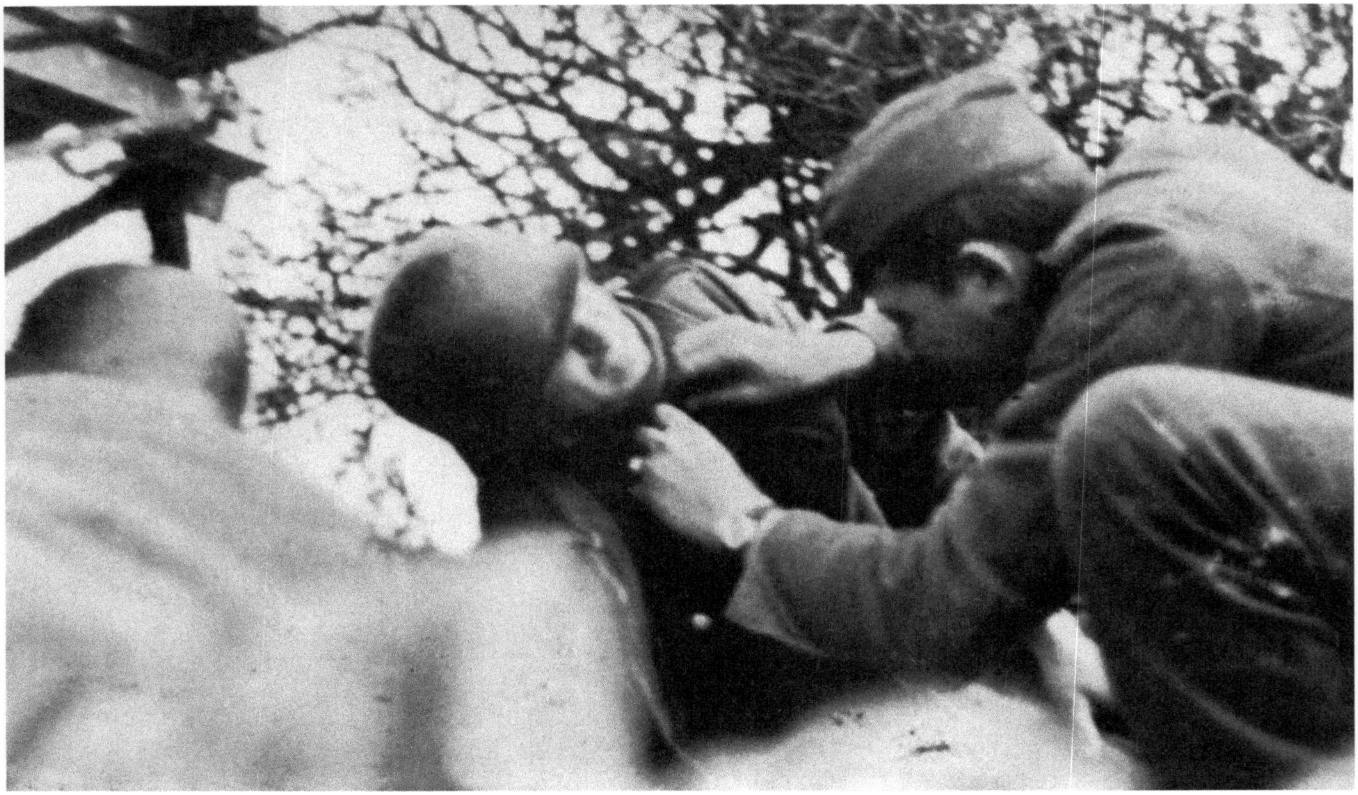

Waffen-SS troops rescue an injured comrade under fire. Waffen-SS injuries in the war in the East are not known but have been estimated at up to 400,000 men.

Waffen-SS Mountain Division *Prinz Eugen* return fire in the mountains of Yugoslavia.

In the closing year of the war ammunition was rationed as supply lines to the German front in the East collapsed.

A sniper targeting Russian reconnaissance troops in the northern sector of the Eastern front.

As the Soviets advanced through Poland in late 1944, the German administration collapsed. Over 600,000 Soviet soldiers died fighting German troops in Poland. A Communist-controlled administration, headed by Bolesław Bierut, was installed by the Soviets in July in Lublin, the first major Polish city to be seized by Russia from Germany.

Units of the Waffen-SS defend the town of Küstrin. The unexpected arrival of Soviet troops at the end of January 1945 at the ancient fortress and garrison town came as a tremendous shock to the German High Command – the Soviets were now only 50 miles from Berlin itself. Two Soviet armies lay siege to the town. Despite this the Germans held out for 60 days but at an appalling human cost – about 5,000 Germans were killed, 9,000 wounded and 6,000 captured. The Russians lost 5,000 killed and 15,000 wounded.

The Battle of Berlin was the last major offensive battle in the East. Intensive street battles left much of the city in ruins. In the defence of Berlin over 100,000 German soldiers were killed before Hitler committed suicide on 30 April 1945. Over 125,000 civilians also died in the battle.

After hostilities had finally ceased on 8 May 1945 nearly one in three Waffen-SS troops were dead or missing in action. To put their mortality rate in context it was the equivalent of all the casualties suffered by the United States military during the entire war.